DEALING WITH
DEATH

*A 4-week course to help junior
highers explore their
feelings about death*

by Gary Wilde

Group®
Loveland, Colorado

Dealing With Death
Copyright © 1991 by Group Publishing, Inc.

First Printing

Credits
Edited by Stephen Parolini
Cover designed by Jill Christopher and DeWain Stoll
Interior designed by Judy Bienick and Jan Aufdemberge
Illustrations by Greg Hollobaugh
Photos on pp. 4 and 45 by David Priest
Photo on p. 29 by Cleo Freelance Photo

ISBN 1-55945-112-2
Printed in the United States of America

CONTENTS

What Happens When You Die?

Help junior highers understand the biblical promise of resurrection.

When Someone Close to You Dies

Help junior highers explore and understand their feelings when someone they care for dies.

Helping a Friend

Help junior highers discover ways to help a grieving friend.

To Live or Die

Help junior highers explore the issue of euthanasia.

DEALING WITH DEATH

To be born is to start on a journey—to the grave. Though death may be tough to face, it's something we live with every moment of our lives. We all face the reality with each heartbeat and each breath—that the beating could stop; that the next breath could be the last.

How do young people deal with this unsavory fact? Popular movies and TV series portray death as an area open to investigation in our society. And many of your junior highers are no doubt caught up in the way death is portrayed by the media.

Our society is obsessed with delaying death as long as possible. And as people seek to escape death, their worries about death grow stronger. Even young teenagers worry greatly about death—see the "Kids' Top Worries" chart in the margin.

Kids' Top Worries

1. Death of a parent
2. Being in a car accident
3. Being in an airplane crash
4. Getting a bad report card
5. Being taken by a stranger
6. Nuclear war
7. Dying

Though fascinated with the subject, society has a hard time facing death squarely. So people spend time, money and energy trying to escape death. With the renewed interest in reincarnation, it seems people are also concerned with what happens after death.

But, eventually, everyone dies. And when people die, how do the survivors cope with the grief? Well . . . sometimes they don't. Psychiatrist Aaron Lazare estimates that 10 to 15 percent of the people who pass through the mental health clinics at Massachusetts General Hospital have—underneath their symptoms—unresolved grief.

Teenagers aren't immune to the ill effects of unhealthy grieving. They often don't know how to respond when a friend or family member dies.

And then there's the issue of "mercy killing." Euthanasia has become a major issue in our society of medical miracles. When, if ever, is it better to allow someone to die rather than keep him or her alive by artificial means?

These are all difficult issues—especially for young teenagers who are going through many physical and emotional changes. Thankfully, you can help your kids with these important issues.

As kids struggle to discover what they believe about the "afterlife," you can give them assurance of Jesus' promise of resurrection. You can help them know that their feelings of sadness and anger are valid; and that God and his people can comfort them. You can teach kids ways to help friends through the grieving process. And you can help kids gain a balanced, biblical perspective on the difficult issue of euthanasia.

This course is your map to help kids deal with death. *Dealing With Death* will help your kids see that Christians can face death with hope.

During this course your students will:
● understand God's gift of life after death;
● explore their emotional and physical pains;
● learn healthy ways to grieve;
● explore practical ways to help a friend grieve;
● discover biblical advice for comforting a friend;
● identify the pros and cons of euthanasia; and
● brainstorm ways to care for terminally ill people.

COURSE OBJECTIVES

HOW TO USE THIS COURSE

ACTIVE LEARNING

Think back on an important lesson you've learned in life. Did you learn it from reading about it? from hearing about it? from something you experienced? Chances are, the most important lessons you've learned came from something you experienced. That's what active learning is—learning by doing. And active learning is a key element in Group's Active Bible Curriculum.

Active learning leads students in doing things that help them understand important principles, messages and ideas. It's a discovery process that helps kids internalize what they learn.

Each lesson section in Group's Active Bible Curriculum plays an important part in active learning:

The **Opener** involves kids in the topic in fun and unusual ways.

The **Action and Reflection** includes an experience designed to evoke specific feelings in the students. This section also processes those feelings through "How did you feel?" questions and applies the message to situations kids face.

The **Bible Application** actively connects the topic with the Bible. It helps kids see how the Bible's message is relevant to the situations they face.

The **Commitment** helps students internalize the Bible's message and commit to make changes in their lives.

The **Closing** funnels the lesson's message into a time of creative reflection and prayer.

When you put all the sections together, you get a lesson that's fun to teach—and kids get messages they'll remember.

BEFORE THE 4-WEEK SESSION

● Read the Introduction, the Course Objectives and This Course at a Glance.

● Decide how you'll publicize the course using the clip art on the Publicity Page (p. 9). Prepare fliers, newsletter articles and posters as needed.

● Look at the Bonus Ideas (p. 46) and decide which ones you'll use.

● Read the opening statements, Objectives and Bible Basis for the lesson. The Bible Basis shows how specific passages relate to junior highers and middle schoolers today.

● Choose which Opener and Closing options to use. Each is appropriate for a different kind of group. The first option is often more active.

● Gather necessary supplies listed in This Lesson at a Glance.

●Read each section of the lesson. Adjust where necessary for your class size and meeting room.

● The approximate minutes listed give you an idea of how long each activity will take. Each lesson is designed to take 35 to 60 minutes. Shorten or lengthen activities as needed to fit your group.

● If you see you're going to have extra time, do an activity or two from the "If You Still Have Time" box or from the Bonus Ideas (p. 46).

● Dive into the activities with the kids. Don't be a spectator. The lesson will be more successful and rewarding to you and your students.

● Death isn't an easy subject to talk about. Kids may feel uncomfortable as they approach this topic. Be sensitive to kids' needs and concerns.

If one of your kids has recently experienced the death of a friend or family member, talk with that student before beginning the course. Powerful feelings are bound to come out during these lessons.

Don't be afraid when kids show their true feelings—that's often when the best learning occurs.

● The answers given after discussion questions are responses your students *might* give. They aren't the only answers or the "right" answers. If needed, use them to spark discussion. Kids won't always say what you wish they'd say. That's why some of the responses given are negative or controversial. If someone responds negatively, don't be shocked. Accept the person, and use the opportunity to explore other angles of the issue.

THIS COURSE AT A GLANCE

Before you dive into the lessons, familiarize yourself with each lesson aim. Then read the scripture passages.
- Study them as a background to the lessons.
- Use them as a basis for your personal devotions.
- Think about how they relate to kids' circumstances today.

LESSON 1: WHAT HAPPENS WHEN YOU DIE?

Lesson Aim: To help junior highers understand the biblical promise of resurrection.

Bible Basis: Job 19:25-27 and 1 Corinthians 15:50-57.

LESSON 2: WHEN SOMEONE CLOSE TO YOU DIES

Lesson Aim: To help junior highers explore and understand their feelings when someone they care for dies.

Bible Basis: Genesis 49:33—50:5 and John 11:32-36.

LESSON 3: HELPING A FRIEND

Lesson Aim: To help junior highers discover ways to help a grieving friend.

Bible Basis: 2 Corinthians 1:3-7 and Revelation 21:1-4.

LESSON 4: TO LIVE OR DIE

Lesson Aim: To help junior highers explore the issue of euthanasia.

Bible Basis: Exodus 20:13 and Job 6:1-11.

PUBLICITY PAGE

Grab your junior highers' attention! Photocopy this page, then cut and paste the art of your choice in your church bulletin or newsletter to advertise this course on dealing with death. Or photocopy and use the ready-made flier as a bulletin insert.

Permission to photocopy the clip art and flier is granted for local church use.

Splash this art on posters, fliers or even postcards! Just add the vital details: the date and time the course begins and where you'll meet.

It's that simple.

DEALING WITH *DEATH*

DEALING WITH
DEATH

A 4-week junior high course to help you deal with your feelings about death

Come to _____

On _____

At _____

Come and discover what happens when you die; why you feel the way you do when someone dies; how to help a grieving friend; and what the Bible says about "mercy killing."

DEALING WITH *DEATH*

WHAT HAPPENS WHEN YOU DIE?

The greatest mystery of life is probably death. No one knows what it's like to die—but everyone dies. Kids today are intrigued by death, so they seek answers to a seemingly impossible question: What happens when you die? With the popularity of beliefs such as reincarnation, kids are getting mixed messages about what happens after they die. From the Bible, kids can learn all they need to know about what happens after death.

To help junior highers understand the biblical promise of resurrection.

LESSON AIM

Students will:
- **play a game to experience the "drudgery" of rebirth in reincarnation;**
- **fill out planning sheets for their own funerals;**
- **commit to living a resurrection life today; and**
- **understand God's gift of life after death.**

OBJECTIVES

Look up the following scriptures. Then read the background paragraphs to see how the passages relate to your junior highers and middle schoolers.

In **Job 19:25-27**, Job affirms his belief that, even after death, he'll see God with his own eyes.

Job was accused by his "friends" of bringing his suffering upon himself as a result of sin in his life. But he knew he'd done nothing wrong. Though his life on earth had become unbearably miserable, Job took comfort in the hope of the resurrection.

Most teenagers are concerned with the "here and now." But

BIBLE BASIS
JOB 19:25-27
1 CORINTHIANS 15:50-57

the experience of Job can remind them that life is very fragile. If our joy in life is tied merely to the unfolding of favorable circumstances, what happens when circumstances turn sour? Or when death itself is the immediate prospect? Our ultimate hope as Christians is in the promise of resurrection to eternal life with God. And teenagers can learn to count on that promise.

In **1 Corinthians 15:50-57**, Paul clearly sets forth the Christian doctrine of the resurrection.

Paul wanted to correct false doctrines about the afterlife that were circulating in the Corinthian church. In this chapter he gives a detailed description of what will occur when Christ returns.

Christian teenagers need to know that the resurrection is not some obscure doctrine tacked onto the Christian faith. Rather, as Paul points out, without the resurrection our faith is useless.

THIS LESSON AT A GLANCE

Section	Minutes	What Students Will Do	Supplies
Opener (Option 1)	5 to 10	**Marshmallow Movie Murder**—Act out simple murder-mystery scenes.	Marshmallows, paper, pencils
(Option 2)		**Deadly Charades**—Play a variation of charades using phrases related to death.	"Charades" box (p. 14), scrap paper, chocolate candies
Action and Reflection	10 to 15	**This Is Your Life, Life, Life . . .**—Experience the concept of reincarnation and contrast it to Jesus' promise of resurrection.	White and black beads, paper bag
Bible Application	10 to 15	**We'll Rise Again**—Learn about the promise of resurrection.	Bibles, "Before You Die" handouts (p. 18), pencils, treats
Commitment	10 to 15	**Live It!**—Commit to living a resurrection life today.	Bibles, "Epitaphs" handouts (p. 19), pencils
Closing (Option 1)	up to 5	**New-Life Joy**—Thank God for the joy of new life in Christ.	Bible
(Option 2)		**Look Out or Look Up?**—Compare the gift of resurrection with the futility of reincarnation.	

The Lesson

☐ OPTION 1: MARSHMALLOW MOVIE MURDER

Form groups of three or four. Give groups each 10 marsh-mallows, a sheet of paper and a pencil. Say: **You've just been hired as writers for a new murder-mystery movie. Your job is to create a unique murder scene that can be filmed. Only the best scene will be used in the movie.**

Have groups each come up with a creative murder scene; for example, a scene where someone is murdered because he or she didn't put enough jelly on a peanut butter and jelly sandwich. Have groups each make notes about their plot and plan to act out the murder scene for the whole group. Tell kids the only rule is that the murder weapons must be marsh-mallows.

Groups might each have one person narrate the story while others act it out. Have fun with this—allow kids to be humor-ous if they want to.

Have groups each act out their murder scene.

After groups have each presented their murder, have kids form a circle.

Ask:

● **How did it feel to act out a murder?** (It was fun; it felt weird; I didn't like it.)

● **How is the portrayal of death in your murder scenes different from death in real life?** (In real life, dead people don't get up after they die; death is much more gruesome in real life; death is scary and sad, not funny.)

Say: **People die all the time in movies. But after the movie scenes are filmed, the dead people simply get up and keep working. They never really die in front of the camera. But what happens when we die in real life? That's the focus of today's lesson.**

☐ OPTION 2: DEADLY CHARADES

Give kids some scrap paper. Say: **We're going to play a game of "deadly charades." Each of you will act out a common phrase that relates to the theme of death. You'll each have 20 seconds to act out your charade for others to guess. If no one guesses your phrase, you'll have to suffer the terrible "crumpled paper" torture. That is, the rest of the class members will crumple up their papers and toss them at you. If someone guesses your phrase, you and the guesser each win a chocolate candy.**

Have the person whose shoes have the most eyelets be first to act out a charade. Show the actor the first phrase in the "Charades" box on page 14. Cover up the other words and phrases so he or she doesn't see them. Then give the actor 20 seconds to silently act out the phrase. If someone figures out the charade, give the actor and the guesser each a chocolate candy. If kids don't figure out the phrase, have them toss lightly toss crumpled papers at the actor.

Give kids each an opportunity to act out a phrase from the list. If you have more than 12 kids, add your own phrases or words to the list.

When kids have each performed a charade, form a circle. Give chocolate candies to kids who didn't get them earlier.

Ask:

● **How did you feel as you did your charade?** (Uncomfortable; confident; silly.)

● **How did you feel if you received the terrible crumpled-paper torture?** (Dumb; nervous; angry.)

● **How is that like the way some people feel when they think about the subject of death?** (Some people feel uncomfortable; some people feel angry.)

Say: **In this activity, you may have felt many different feelings, such as anger, guilt or fear. Thinking about death brings about some of the same feelings. Many of those feelings come from not knowing what happens when someone dies. Today we're going to let the Bible help us learn what happens when we die.**

Charades

- dead duck
- dead in the water
- dead head
- dead tired
- working myself to death
- death by chocolate
- die laughing
- diehard
- death bed
- death-defying
- dying to know
- wake the dead
- _____
- _____
- _____
- _____

ACTION AND REFLECTION

(10 to 15 minutes)

THIS IS YOUR LIFE, LIFE, LIFE . . .

Say: **Eventually, everyone dies. And because death is inevitable, people are curious about it. People wonder what happens after death. One common belief is that people are reincarnated, but the Bible doesn't teach us about reincarnation; it teaches us the truth—about resurrection. Though they may sound somewhat similar, reincarnation is much different from resurrection. Let's find out what reincarnation is.**

Tell students to each imagine that instead of being given one life to live, they have to live as many lives as it takes to become perfect. Put some beads in a paper bag, one-fourth white beads and three-fourths black beads. (You could use black and white jelly beans or black and white squares of paper instead of beads.) Place the bag at the front of the room.

Have students form a line and pass by the bag. As they pass, have them each take five beads without looking. Tell kids who have all white beads they're "perfect" and may sit down. Have the other kids each go through the line again, drop their previously chosen beads back into the bag, and pick five new beads.

Have kids continue to go through the line as many as five times. Few will likely have picked five white beads.

Ask:

● **How easy was it to collect five white beads? Explain.** (Very easy, I picked them on the first try; difficult, I always had at least one black bead.)

● **How much control did you have in getting the beads you wanted?** (None; it was all luck.)

Say: **The theory of reincarnation is a lot like this game. In reincarnation, people must be reborn again and again in their search to finally become perfect. How well people do in a particular "life" determines their advantages as they start the next "round." Some people who believe in reincarnation feel bound by the actions of past lives—with little hope of escape.**

Ask:

● **How did you feel as you tried to get five white beads?** (Frustrated; angry; hopeful.)

Say: **Reincarnation is a popular belief of New-Agers and of Eastern religions such as Hinduism. But the Bible teaches us about a different kind of rebirth.**

Give kids each a white bead. Say: **When Jesus died for our sins, he gave us the promise of resurrection. There's no "cosmic lottery" system to determine whether you'll end up with five white beads someday. God's promise is both simple and powerful: Someday, when Christ returns, believers in Christ will be given new heavenly bodies and we'll live eternally with Jesus. Just as you were each given one white bead as a gift, so resurrection is given to each of us as a gift from God.**

WE'LL RISE AGAIN

Say: **Job suffered many terrible things in his life. Yet in the midst of his terrible suffering, he still hoped in God.** Have someone read aloud Job 19:25-27.

● **How does Job's hope in resurrection make you feel?** (Great; confident; hopeful.)

Say: **Even though Job didn't understand what the circumstances would be, he felt sure he'd see God after he died. Death is still a big unknown for us, too, because we don't fully comprehend what our new bodies will be like. But we can feel comforted knowing death won't take us farther away from God—but closer to him.**

Give kids each a Bible, a pencil and a "Before You Die" handout (p. 18). This handout may bring up kids' concerns about suicide. It's not uncommon for junior highers to think about suicide. If kids do bring up the issue, or if you sense kids are struggling with suicidal feelings, use this opportunity to guide kids toward positive feelings about living. Kids will be easily turned off by a "life's great!" speech. Instead, help kids see how even in the tough times, God is with them and can

I Corenthins 15:50-57

BIBLE APPLICATION
(10 to 15 minutes)

help them through. Encourage kids to support one another through the tough times, too.

Say: **We don't know when we'll die, but we can learn from the Bible how we can be prepared for that time. This handout will help you think about things you should know before you die. In a couple minutes, you'll form pairs to discuss the handouts.**

After six minutes or so, have kids form pairs to discuss their handouts. During the discussion time, leave the room and bring back a cake or other treat. Then serve it to your surprised kids.

Ask:

● **How did you feel as you were completing and discussing your handouts?** (Depressed; sad; quiet.)

● **How did your mood change when you saw the treat I brought in?** (We got excited; we were happy.)

Say: **When we think about death, we often feel depressed or quiet. Yet, just as you were excited to see the treat, we'll be surprised and excited when we're resurrected and meet Jesus face to face. And the surprise will be much better than this food!**

COMMITMENT
(10 to 15 minutes)

LIVE IT!

Give kids each a pencil and an "Epitaphs" handout (p. 19). Say: **When our physical bodies die, we'll each probably be buried in a grave. What will your epitaph (gravestone) say about you? Take a couple minutes to complete the top half of your handout. Think about how people will remember you after you die. Will they remember your faith? your good works? your joy?**

Give kids a couple minutes; then read aloud Romans 8:10-11.

Ask:

● **Does your epitaph describe a strong spiritual life? Why or why not?** (Don't force kids to answer, but encourage them to think about the question.)

● **How can you live each day with "resurrection joy"?** (By praying daily; by loving God; by trusting God.)

Form pairs. Have students each read and complete the second half of the "Epitaphs" handout for their partner, tear it off and present it to the partner.

Then form a circle. Have kids each read one thing their partner wrote about them on the handout. Then say: **We can count on God's promise of a resurrected life with him. But we can also begin to live our resurrection lives today— showing our love for God in practical ways while we have our earthly bodies.**

Have kids each tell one thing they'll do (or are doing) that can help them live resurrection lives. Kids might suggest things such as praying daily, counting on God's love, telling friends about Christ or worshiping regularly.

Table Talk

The Table Talk activity in this course helps junior highers and middle schoolers talk with their parents about death.

If you choose to use the Table Talk activity, this is a good time to show students the "Table Talk" handout (p. 20). Ask them to spend time with their parents completing it.

Before kids leave, give them each them each a "Table Talk" handout to take home, or tell them you'll send it to their parents.

Or use the Table Talk idea found in the Bonus Ideas (p. 47) for a meeting based on the handout.

☐ OPTION 1: NEW-LIFE JOY

Read aloud Ephesians 2:1-5. Say: **Without Christ, we're truly dead. But when we become Christians, we gain new life in Christ and the promise of life after death—eternal life with Christ.**

Close in prayer, allowing kids each an opportunity to thank God for the promise of resurrection and the joy of new life in him.

☐ OPTION 2: LOOK OUT OR LOOK UP?

Say: **Pantomime with me the following situation. We're walking along a sidewalk.** (Pantomime walking and encourage kids to do likewise.) **We're looking at the clouds, wondering what they're really like.** (Pantomime looking up.) **Suddenly, we trip on a huge crack in the sidewalk. We fall with a crash.** (Pantomime tripping and falling.)

As we lie on the ground in pain, two strangers come up. One says: "Next time, try to be more careful" and walks away. The other reaches down his hand and says, "Here, let me help you up." (Pantomime being helped up.)

Reincarnation is a lot like the first stranger: There's little comfort in being told to "be careful next time." But God has the ultimate comfort for us: He offers us the gift of eternal life.

Have volunteers close in prayer, thanking God for the promise of resurrection.

CLOSING
(up to 5 minutes)

If You Still Have Time . . .

Is Death the Answer?—Have kids seriously discuss the issue of suicide. Be sensitive in this discussion if you know of someone who's committed suicide. Allow kids to express their feelings about whether they've ever thought about committing suicide. Use scriptures such as Psalm 31:24; 34:19; Proverbs 3:5; and Philippians 4:7 to spark discussion on the value of life. Help kids see that although things can be tough sometimes, God can always help us through.

Death in the Media—Have kids discuss how death and afterlife are portrayed in popular TV shows, movies and music. Then have kids compare the media's perspective on life after death with the biblical view of resurrection.

BEFORE YOU DIE

Thinking about death isn't easy for anybody. But take a few minutes to complete this handout anyway. Then find a partner and talk about your completed handout.

● Name

● Age

● How do you think you'll die?

● Who will make your funeral arrangements?

● Who will be the most important people at your funeral?

● What do you want said at your funeral?

● Read 2 Corinthians 5:1-9. What does this passage tell you about death? How does that make you feel about dying?

● Read John 11: 25-26. How can you count on the resurrection Jesus promised?

● Will your funeral be a joyful or sad event? Explain.

● To end this handout on a happy note, read 1 John 3:1. List two reasons you're glad to be called a child of God. Then list two reasons you're glad to be alive today!

I'm glad to be a child of God because . . .

1.

2.

I'm glad to be alive today because . . .

1.

2.

EPITAPHS

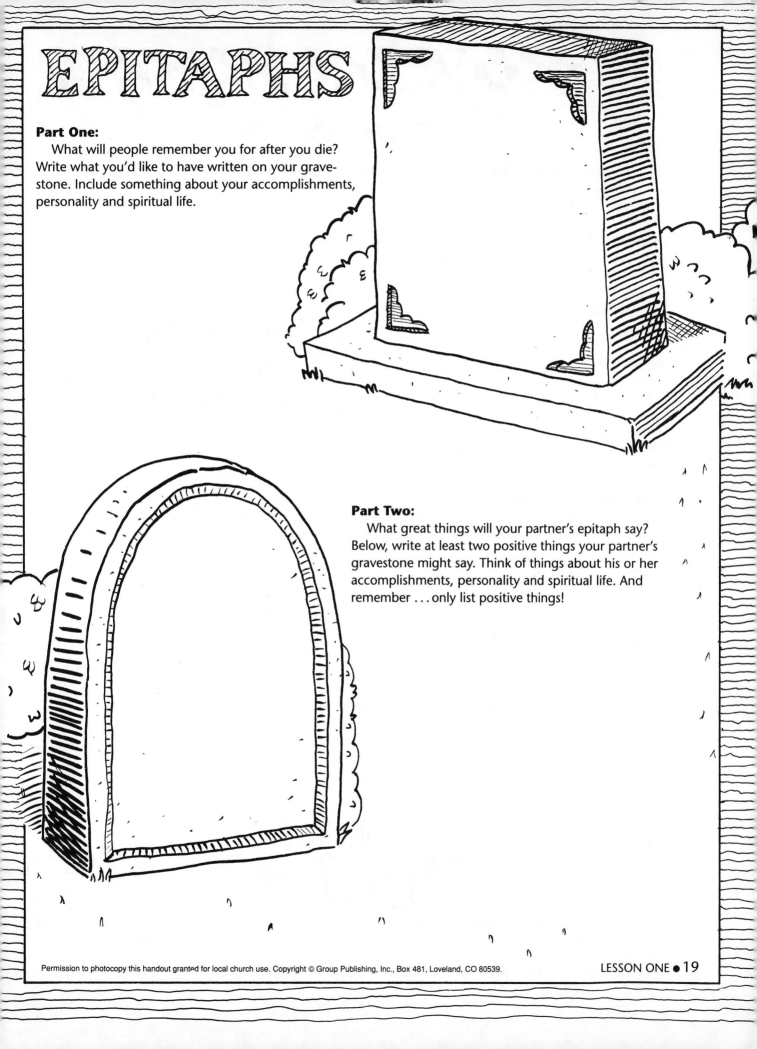

Part One:

What will people remember you for after you die? Write what you'd like to have written on your gravestone. Include something about your accomplishments, personality and spiritual life.

Part Two:

What great things will your partner's epitaph say? Below, write at least two positive things your partner's gravestone might say. Think of things about his or her accomplishments, personality and spiritual life. And remember . . . only list positive things!

Table Talk

To the Parent: We're involved in a junior high course at church called *Dealing With Death*. We'd like you and your son or daughter to spend some time discussing this important topic. Use this "Table Talk" page to help you.

Parent

Complete the following sentences:
- When I was a teenager, the most difficult experience with death I had was . . .
- Death scares me because . . .
- Death doesn't scare me because . . .
- When someone close to me dies, I feel . . .
- I've helped a friend grieve by . . .

Junior higher

Complete the following sentences:
- What I struggle with most about death is . . .
- Death scares me because . . .
- Death doesn't scare me because . . .
- If someone close to me died, I'd feel . . .
- I can help a friend grieve by . . .

Parent and junior higher

Separately complete the following sentences on sheets of paper. After you've each completed the sentences, meet together and share what you wrote. Talk about the similarities and differences in how you completed the sentences.
- The first death I remember was . . .
- When this person (or animal) died, I felt . . .
- The thought of attending a funeral makes me feel . . .
- When someone I know dies, I think about . . .
- I cope with death (or other big loss) by . . .
- I know I'm grieving in a healthy way when . . .

Talk together about how you feel about Jesus' promise of life after death for those who love him. Read together John 14:2-3 and 1 Corinthians 15:21-26. Discuss the passages and what they say about life after death.

DEALING WITH *DEATH*

WHEN SOMEONE CLOSE TO YOU DIES

Sometime during their life, kids must each deal with the death of someone they care about. When someone close to them dies, kids must deal with all sorts of feelings at once—feelings they may not know how to handle. Yet kids can learn how to grieve in a healthy way.

To help junior highers explore and understand their feelings when someone they care for dies.

LESSON AIM

OBJECTIVES

Students will:
- participate in an activity to experience the physical aspects of grief;
- explore their own emotional and physical pains;
- examine how three biblical characters grieved;
- learn healthy ways to grieve; and
- discuss honest feelings about significant loss.

BIBLE BASIS
GENESIS 49:33—50:5
JOHN 11:32-36

Look up the following scriptures. Then read the background paragraphs to see how the passages relate to your junior highers and middle schoolers.

In **Genesis 49:33—50:5**, Jacob dies, and his son Joseph must handle the burial arrangements.

When Jacob knew his death was near, he gathered all his sons around him and blessed them. His family was no doubt filled with anticipatory grief, yet the reality of death was faced squarely. Joseph grieved openly for his dead father, with weeping.

Teenagers can see in this passage that death must be accepted as a part of life. But that doesn't mean feelings of sadness should be denied or covered up. Joseph's response shows that the death of a loved one is always devastating—we grieve and cry. Yet we can recover. When the days of mourning have passed, we go on with life.

In **John 11:32-36**, Jesus visits the tomb of his friend Lazarus to raise him from the dead.

When Jesus arrived at the burial site, he was moved by the scene of mourning and weeping around him. Jesus, too, apparently felt the sting of loss, because he also wept.

Teenagers instinctively know that when someone close dies, the survivors feel the hurt. But they may wonder just how appropriate it is to acknowledge and express that hurt in the presence of others. Jesus is their example here: Even the son of God weeps in public!

THIS LESSON AT A GLANCE

Section	Minutes	What Students Will Do	Supplies
Opener (Option 1)	5 to 10	**Slow-Motion Skits**—Create commercials and act them out in slow motion.	
(Option 2)		**Painful Shuffle**—Determine losses that are easy and difficult to deal with.	3×5 cards, pencils
Action and Reflection	10 to 15	**Sensation-al Olympics**—Participate in activities to help them understand feelings associated with grief.	Crackers, masking tape, blindfolds, newsprint, marker, "Sensations" hand-outs (p. 27), pencils, candy
Bible Application	10 to 15	**Three Guys Who Grieved**—Explore the grief three biblical characters felt.	Bibles, posterboard, markers
Commitment	10 to 15	**Facing Feelings**—Learn how to face feelings honestly.	"Good Grief" handouts (p. 28), pencils
Closing (Option 1)	up to 5	**Empty Chair**—Remember or imagine the loss of a loved one, and support one another.	
(Option 2)		**Pain and Gain**—Discuss how the pain of grief can help them grow.	

Note: This lesson covers a particularly sensitive subject: dealing with the death of someone close. Kids may become upset if a friend or family member has recently died. Comfort them with hugs and let them cry—that's the whole point of this lesson. If there have been recent tragedies in your church or in kids' schools, you may spend much of this lesson talking about kids' feelings. Your students may feel uncomfortable if someone begins to cry. Encourage them to talk through their feelings. They may surprise you with their caring attitudes and concerns for classmates who are upset.

The Lesson

☐ OPTION 1: SLOW-MOTION SKITS

Form groups of no more than three. Have groups each make up a 10- to 15-second commercial for a funeral home. Tell kids they can make the commercial funny or serious. Go around and help kids create their commercials.

After five minutes or so, call time. Say: **Now you'll each get to perform your commercial for the whole group. But there's one problem: When the commercials were filmed, the camera got stuck on super-slow motion. So you'll need to act out your commercials in slow motion.**

Have groups each present their commercial. Then form a circle.

Ask:

● **How did you feel as you tried to do your commercial in slow motion?** (I felt silly; I thought it was fun.)

● **Have you ever felt like you were moving in slow motion in real life? Why or why not?** (Yes, sometimes I feel that way when I'm tired; yes, sometimes I feel that way when I've got too much to do.)

Say: **Life can sometimes seem to move in slow motion. A sensation of being in "slow motion" often accompanies the initial shock of grief when someone close dies. This sense of unreality can last a few days.**

The feelings of being in slow motion, and many other feelings, are normal for people grieving about someone who's died. Today we'll take a look at healthy ways to deal with the feelings we have when someone we care for dies.

☐ OPTION 2: PAINFUL SHUFFLE

Give kids each five 3×5 cards and a pencil. Have kids write on each card a different experience of loss they've had; for example, death of a friend, loss of an object, death of a pet, loss of a parent in divorce, loss of a friend because of moving away. Tell kids these losses can be anything from a serious event to a light, funny event. Tell kids not to list names on their cards.

Then collect and shuffle the cards. Deal out five cards to each student. Say: **Now, read your cards and find the loss that's easiest to deal with and the loss that's most difficult to deal with.**

Collect the "easiest" and "most difficult" cards from each student and place them in separate piles.

Then have volunteers take turns reading a card from each pile. Kids may laugh at some of the items in the "easiest" pile. That's okay. Sometimes, humor helps kids relax so they can talk about serious subjects such as death. Allow kids to giggle or laugh, but be prepared to talk about kids' uneasy feelings if someone laughs inappropriately.

After all the "easiest" and "most difficult" cards are read, ask:

● **How did you feel as you thought about what to write on your cards?** (Anxious; sad; fine.)

● **How did you feel when people read the cards aloud?** (Upset; anxious; happy.)

● **How is that like the way people feel when they experience loss?** (Some people are upset; some people are fine; some people feel anxious.)

● **What does this activity tell us about the losses people have?** (Some losses are more important to people than others; everyone seems to have experienced some kind of loss.)

Say: **Everybody experiences loss and grief to some degree. You may have had a devastating loss of a family member or close friend. Or you may not have experienced the loss of someone close to you. The feelings we have when we experience the "most difficult" kinds of losses, such as the death of a family member or friend, are tough to deal with. Today we'll explore the feelings we have and learn how to grieve in a healthy way.**

Table Talk Follow-Up

If you sent the "Table Talk" handout (p. 20) to parents last week, discuss students' reactions to the activity. Ask volunteers to share what they learned from the discussion with their parents.

ACTION AND REFLECTION

(10 to 15 minutes)

SENSATION-AL OLYMPICS

Say: **Before we talk about grief, we're going to participate in a unique competition. There will be five different events, and prizes for the winners of each event.**

Lead kids through each of the following events. Award a candy prize to the winner of each event. You may want to limit the prizes to one per person.

The first event is the "Cracker Crunch." Give kids each five saltine crackers, and see who can eat them all first. Tell kids they must eat one at a time and must swallow one before eating another.

The second game is "Blue-in-the-Face." Have kids each sit in a chair and see who can hold his or her breath the longest. Warn kids to stop holding their breath when they begin to feel dizzy.

Have kids take off their shoes for the third game, called "At Arms' Length." Have kids each stand with their arms parallel to the floor, holding a shoe in each hand. Award a prize to the person who can hold this position the longest. This could go on a while, so you may want to call time and award more than one prize.

For the fourth game, "What, Me Dizzy?," use masking tape to make a straight line on the floor about 10 feet long. Then, one at a time, spin kids around three times and have them each attempt to follow the straight line within a five-second time limit. Award a prize to each person who successfully walks the line without wandering off the masking tape.

For the final game, "Prize Search," blindfold kids and place a candy prize somewhere in the room. Don't tell kids where the prize is. On "go," have kids feel their way around the room attempting to find the prize. If no one finds the prize after a minute or so, call time. Make sure kids don't hurt themselves while wandering around.

After the games are completed, award candy prizes to kids who didn't win any during the games. Then form a circle.

Ask the following questions and write kids' answers on newsprint:

● **How did you feel after the "Cracker Crunch" activity? Describe your physical feelings and emotions.** (I had a dry throat; I felt tightness in my throat; I had to swallow a lot; I felt bad that I didn't win.)

● **How did you feel after the "Blue-in-the-Face" activity?** (I was out of breath; I felt lightheaded; I was disappointed.)

● **How did you feel after the "At Arms' Length" activity?** (My muscles were sore; my arms ached; I was out of energy.)

● **How did you feel after the "What, Me Dizzy?" activity?** (I felt silly; I felt out of control; I felt dizzy or disoriented.)

● **How did you feel in the "Prize Search" activity?** (Helpless; lost; unsure where I was.)

● **Look at the answers on the newsprint. How are all the physical and emotional feelings listed here like the feelings people have when someone they love dies?** (They get physically sick; their throats get dry; they feel disoriented; they feel tired.)

Say: **The way you felt after each activity is similar to the way we feel when we first hear about a friend's death. We may get a dry throat, feel dizzy, become tired or feel lost. These are all real feelings and they're valid feelings.**

And just as the physical feelings we had in these activities were real, so are the emotional responses we have when someone close to us dies.

Give kids each a "Sensations" handout (p. 27) and a pencil. Have kids each complete the handout.

Then form a circle and have volunteers tell what they wrote for each feeling on the handout. Encourage kids to participate, but don't force them to reveal their answers.

Say: **We've each had experiences with many or all of the feelings on the handout. And those feelings are real. It's okay to express your feelings when you grieve. Let's take a look at three biblical characters and see how they grieved.**

THREE GUYS WHO GRIEVED

Form groups of no more than three. Give groups each a Bible, a sheet of posterboard and some markers. Assign groups each one of the following scripture passages: Genesis 49:33—50:5; 2 Samuel 18:31—19:4; or John 11:32-36. Have groups each read their passage. Then have groups each create a poster depicting the situation in the passage—and showing how the main character dealt with grief. For example, one group might draw a picture of Jesus crying as he's standing near Lazarus' tomb.

Then have groups each present their poster, briefly explaining the passage and how the main character dealt with grief.

Then ask:

● **What do these stories tell us about showing our feelings when someone close to us dies?** (It's okay to cry; we should show our feelings.)

Say: **Learning to grieve in a healthy way isn't easy. We'll each have different responses to feelings of pain and loss. That's okay—no two people are alike. Let's see how we each deal with our feelings.**

FACING FEELINGS

Give kids each a "Good Grief" handout (p. 28) and a pencil. Have kids each complete the handout. Then form pairs and have partners talk about their completed handouts and the discussion questions at the bottom of the page.

● **Why is it important to express your feelings when you're upset?** (Because if you don't, you'll just make yourself feel worse; because that's the best way to get over your feelings.)

● **Why do people deny or suppress their feelings?** (Because they want to look strong; because they don't want to look stupid; because they don't think it's okay to express them.)

Ask kids to each say one thing they'll do to grieve in a healthy way. Then have kids each tell their partner one positive thing about how the partner completed the handout; for example, "It's good that you show your feelings" or "I know you can learn to show your anger in a good way."

Form a circle. Say: **When someone close to us dies, we feel many different feelings. It's okay to express those feelings. And with God's love and support from friends, we can grieve in a healthy way—and then get on with our lives.**

☐ OPTION 1: EMPTY CHAIR

Place an empty chair in the center of the circle. Say: **Look at this empty chair and remember or imagine the loss of a loved one. As you think about this person's death, concentrate on your feelings. Remember: It's okay to cry and be upset. When Jesus learned of the death of his friend Lazarus, he cried.**

Have kids put their arms around each other for a group hug. Close in prayer, allowing time for silent prayer. Be available for kids who might still be upset when class is over.

☐ OPTION 2: PAIN AND GAIN

Ask:

● **What does the phrase "no pain, no gain" mean?** (You have to work for what you get; if you don't hurt, you're not working hard enough.)

Say: **While that phrase may not truly be appropriate for grieving, it does have truth in it. When we're hurt or in pain, we can't see much beyond the hurt. But afterward, we're stronger and wiser. The pain we feel helps us gain a new perspective on ourselves and those around us.**

Have volunteers close in prayer, thanking God for giving us feelings to express when someone close to us dies. Then have kids go around and hug at least three other people.

Be available for kids who might continue to be upset even when class is over.

CLOSING
(up to 5 minutes)

If You Still Have Time . . .

Grief Counseling—Invite a pastor or counselor to attend the meeting. Have him or her briefly discuss the process of grieving. Allow kids to ask questions about the nature of grieving.

Grief and Relief—Have kids each draw and explain a picture or symbol showing how they feel when someone close to them dies. Form a circle. Have kids each hand their picture to the person on their left. Then have kids each write an encouraging or uplifting note on the back of the picture they've been given; for example, "Hang in there, God loves you" or "It's okay to cry."

Then have kids return the pictures to their owners. Encourage kids to keep the pictures as reminders that it's okay to cry and that there's hope in the middle of pain.

SENSATIONS

For each of the feelings listed below, write about a situation when you felt that feeling. For example, under "sadness," you might describe how you felt sad when a close friend moved away. You won't have to reveal your answers if you don't want to.

Sadness

Anger (at God or people)

Doubt

Fear

Denial (this isn't really happening)

Frustration

Depression

Worry

Good Grief

Read each of the following statements, then circle your response.

When I'm upset . . .	I keep my feelings to myself.
	I let my feelings show.
When something angers me . . .	I pretend I'm fine when I'm around others.
	I let people know how I feel.
If I want to be alone . . .	I usually can't get away from friends.
	I ask my friends to give me space.
If I get angry at God . . .	I hide my anger.
	I let someone know how I feel.
When I'm in pain . . .	I grit my teeth and smile anyway.
	I cry.

Discussion Questions:
- Compare your answers with your partner's. How are you alike? How are you different?
- Do you always react in the same way to painful situations?
- What one thing might you do to have a healthier approach to grieving?

LESSON 3

HELPING A FRIEND

Friendship is one of the most important aspects of a junior higher's life. Kids want to have friends to spend time with and share dreams with. But sometimes, a friend's dream is shattered by tragedy. Junior highers are still learning what it means to be a friend. Most don't yet have the skills to reach out to someone in pain. But they can learn.

LESSON AIM

To help junior highers discover ways to help a grieving friend.

OBJECTIVES

Students will:
● **think of ways to help each other feel happy;**
● **explore practical ways to help a friend grieve;**
● **discover biblical advice for comforting a friend; and**
● **learn what it means to be empathic toward a hurting friend.**

BIBLE BASIS

2 CORINTHIANS 1:3-7
REVELATION 21:1-4

Look up the following scriptures. Then read the background paragraphs to see how the passages relate to your junior highers and middle schoolers.

In **2 Corinthians 1:3-7**, Paul praises God's comforting ways.

Paul says we can offer comfort to others because we ourselves have been comforted by God. This message implies that we build up a "reserve" of comfort out of which we can help others who are hurting.

Through this passage, teenagers can be reminded that suffering, grief or difficult times can have positive benefits. Good can come from our suffering when we use it to understand the suffering of others—and to help others through it.

In **Revelation 21:1-4**, John describes his vision of the new Jerusalem.

The book of Revelation is full of figurative language and symbolic grandeur. But John offers encouragement and comfort for future, unknown times. He reminds us that our earthly lives are nothing compared to the life in the new Jerusalem with Christ.

This passage gives us a glimpse of heaven. Teenagers can be encouraged by knowing that, as scary as death is, it doesn't last forever for those who love God. In heaven, there will be no more death—and no more grief. Kids can learn to count on God's promises to wipe away all grief, pain and tears.

THIS LESSON AT A GLANCE

Section	Minutes	What Students Will Do	Supplies
Opener (Option 1)	5 to 10	**Tangled Feelings**—Unravel yarn, symbolizing their feelings.	Yarn
(Option 2)		**Sticking With the Pain**—Listen to "painful" music and discuss how important it is to hang in there with friends.	Tape player, cassette of unpopular music
Action and Reflection	10 to 15	**What Can I Say?**—Say things to help each other be happy.	Construction paper, markers
Bible Application	10 to 15	**The Task of Mourning**—Study scripture passages and develop practical ways to help someone mourn.	Bibles, cotton balls, "From Mourning to Dancing" handouts (p. 37), pencils
Commitment	10 to 15	**Reflecting**—Learn reflective listening.	Cotton balls
Closing (Option 1)	up to 5	**Active Silence**—Support each other as they think about personal grief.	Bible
(Option 2)		**Prayer Circle**—Pray for people suffering from grief.	

The Lesson

☐ OPTION 1: TANGLED FEELINGS

Before the meeting, create tangled piles of yarn. Take equal lengths of yarn (at least 20 feet) and twist, roll and tie them up so they become a tangled mess.

Form groups of no more than four. Give groups each a tangled pile of yarn.

OPENER
(5 to 10 minutes)

Say: **You have three minutes to unravel your yarn. The group that unravels the yarn first, or has the most yarn unraveled, in three minutes will be the winner. Each group member must participate in the unraveling process. If you break your yarn, you'll be disqualified. Ready? Go!**

If no group finishes unraveling its yarn within the time limit, measure the length of each partially unraveled mess of yarn to determine the winner.

Ask:

● **How easy was it to unravel the yarn?** (Not very easy; difficult; easy.)

● **How is the tangled yarn like people's feelings when someone close dies?** (People are all confused; people have lots of mixed feelings all tossed together.)

Say: **When someone dies, the people close to him or her react with lots of different feelings. We learned last week how we can deal with those feelings in healthy ways. But what if a friend is dealing with the pain of a loved one's death? How can we help a friend untangle the mess of feelings he or she probably has? Today we'll focus on the the things a grieving person has to do to cope with loss, and ways we, as friends, can help in that process.**

☐ OPTION 2: STICKING WITH THE PAIN

Ask your kids if they'd like to spend a few minutes listening to music. If they say no, tell them you'd like them to hear some music anyway. Play a cassette your kids won't like; for example, polka music, marching-band music, big-band music, classical music or Gregorian chants. Choose music that will bring the most shouts of "turn that off" or "that's terrible!"

After a minute or so, ask for a show of hands indicating how many kids would like to hear more. Expect groans and plenty of "no thank yous." Continue playing the music. After a couple more minutes, stop the tape.

Ask:

● **Would you leave the room right now if you could? Why or why not?** (Yes, I hate that sound; yes, I'd rather listen to good music; no, I like the music.)

● **How is hanging around and listening to this unpleasant music like hanging around to support a grieving friend?** (It's not always easy to stay with a hurting friend; friends who are upset aren't always pleasant to listen to.)

Say: **One of the hardest things about helping a grieving person is sticking around someone who has "unpleasant" or "unpopular" feelings. The feelings our friend may have—sadness, anger, guilt, fear—may make us want to close our ears or leave the room. We may be tempted to change the subject when our friend starts talking about things that really hurt inside. The person who is best able to help is the one who is willing to stick close to the pain. Today we'll learn practical ways to "stick around."**

WHAT CAN I SAY?

Form pairs. Say: **You each have one minute to tell your partner things that will help make him or her happy. You may not touch your partner or move around the room—you may only talk. You don't have to talk the whole time, but you must do your best to make your partner happier than he or she was before you started talking.**

Have partners each take a turn spending one minute trying to make their partner happy. Then have partners discuss how successful they were at making each other happy.

Ask:

● **How easy was it to make your partner happy? Explain.** (Very easy, I knew what would make him or her laugh; difficult, everything I said sounded negative.)

● **How is this activity like trying to cheer up a person who has just lost a loved one?** (It's similar because it's not easy to make a person happy; it's much different, this was easy but cheering up a friend isn't.)

Say: **Now, you'll each have another chance to make your friend happier, but you may not say a word. You must do something for your partner that will brighten his or her day.**

Give partners each one minute to do something for their partner; for example, give a backrub or get a glass of water.

Then ask:

● **How easy was it to make your partner happy this time? Explain.** (Very easy, the backrub was a positive thing to do; somewhat easy, I couldn't think of much to do.)

Say: **Sometimes we can help people feel good by the things we say. Other times, it's what we do that can help people feel better. And sometimes, no matter what we try, we can't help a friend who's upset or sad.**

● **Have you ever tried to say "just the right thing" to a hurting or grieving person? What happened?** (Yes, it helped him feel better; yes, it made her upset.)

● **How do you feel when you're around someone who's hurting?** (Sad; uncomfortable; fine.)

● **Why is it so tough to know what to say or do?** (Because we don't really know how the person is feeling; because people who are upset don't want to listen.)

Give kids each a sheet of construction paper and a marker. Have kids each draw a "smiley face" on one side of the paper and a "frown face" on the other.

Form a circle. Say: **I'm going to read things people might say or do to help you if you were grieving. If you think the action or words would help you deal with a painful situation, hold the paper against you with the happy face showing out. If you think the action or words wouldn't help, hold the paper so the sad face shows out.**

Read the following list and pause to allow kids' responses:

● **Helping you do your daily chores around the home.**

- Saying "I really care about you."
- Inviting you to go to a movie.
- Saying "Things will get better."
- Telling you jokes.
- Going with you to see a counselor or pastor.
- Listening to you.
- Saying "It's not your fault."
- Saying "Don't cry about it."
- Spending time with you.

Ask:

- **What did you notice about the way people reacted to each item?** (We had different responses; we had similar responses.)

Say: **As we can tell from this exercise, people respond differently to things we say or do for them. Simply "finding the right words to say" isn't the only way to help a friend. Grieving friends need us to acknowledge their pain and remain with them in it. We can't take the hurt away, but we can empathize with them and offer comforting words. Empathizing means feeling what someone else is feeling. By empathizing, we're able to better understand how to respond to hurting friends.**

BIBLE APPLICATION
(10 to 15 minutes)

THE TASK OF MOURNING

Have someone read aloud 2 Corinthians 1:3-7.
Ask:

- **What does this passage tell us about comforting others?** (We can comfort others because we've been comforted by God.)

Give kids each a handful of cotton balls. Say: **Each of these cotton balls represents a time God comforted you. Think about ways you've felt comforted by God.**

Have kids each describe one or more times they felt comforted by God. For example, kids might say, "I felt comforted when God answered my prayer about my friend" or "I felt comforted when God helped me overcome my fear." Have kids hold on to their cotton balls until the Commitment activity.

Then say: **God's example of comfort can teach us how to comfort others. Let's think of practical ways we can reach out to people who are mourning the loss of a friend.**

Give kids each a "From Mourning to Dancing" handout (p. 37), a pencil and a Bible. Have kids each complete the handout. Then have kids pair up and talk about their completed handouts. Have kids report back to the whole group what they learned from their discussions.

Say: **Now that we've thought of practical ways to help a grieving friend, let's zero in on one key thing that'll always be part of our approach to someone who's hurting— good listening. We can listen while trying to understand what the other person feels. We call this empathic listening.**

Ask:

● **What is empathic listening?** (Listening as the other person would; trying to feel the way the other person does as you listen.)

Say: **When we listen "beneath" the words to hear the person's feelings, we're listening with empathy. It takes commitment and practice to learn to listen this way. But it's worth it.**

REFLECTING

Say: **One way to practice empathic listening is to use reflective statements. This means responding to another person's words with a statement that sums up the feelings you hear expressed. Doing this shows you're listening intently to the other person's feelings.**

I'm going to give you an example of a reflective statement. Then I'll read a few more statements and ask volunteers to practice reflecting those statements back to me.

If a friend says "Sometimes I wish my dad were still here to help me plan for college," you might respond by saying "You feel sad because your dad isn't around to give you advice, right?" Now let's try a few more . . .

Read aloud each of the following statements one at a time, and have volunteers respond with reflective statements based on each one. Ask for a couple reflections for each statement.

● **It's been a year since my brother died, but it's still tough for me to walk past his bedroom door.**

● **My mom has cancer. She only has only a few weeks to live. I just don't know what we'll do without her.**

● **I'm angry at my dad. He should've never told me about Grandpa's cancer. I have enough problems; I don't want to think about Grandpa dying.**

● **I'm angry at Jerry. Why did he have to go and kill himself anyway?**

● **Those kids were so careless. I told them not to drive so fast! What am I going to do now that my best friends are dead?**

After practicing the reflective statements, have kids form a circle. Say: **Listening and comforting help friends through the difficult times of mourning. In times of need, we can all use friends. But even when we're not in need, friendship comforts us and makes us strong.**

Make sure kids still have their cotton balls from the Bible Application activity. Have kids each give one cotton ball to at least four other people. Each time they give someone a cotton ball, have kids each say one reason they value that person's friendship. For example, someone might say, "I appreciate your sense of humor" or "Your caring attitude helps me feel good."

C O M M I T M E N T
(10 to 15 minutes)

CLOSING
(up to 5 minutes)

☐ OPTION 1: ACTIVE SILENCE

Tell students they'll have two minutes of silence to think about the issue of grief. Form pairs and have each pair find a place in the room to sit quietly. Ask kids to each think about something that is hurting them or a friend. After two minutes, have partners briefly pray for each other. Then read Revelation 21:1-4 aloud as a closing.

☐ OPTION 2: PRAYER CIRCLE

Have students form a circle and hold hands. Ask kids to describe situations they know about in which someone is grieving or sad. Or have kids each tell something they're saddened by. Then have kids take turns praying for the specific concerns.

If You Still Have Time . . .

Listen and Respond—Form groups of no more than three. Have kids brainstorm things they can do to help someone who's upset or grieving. For example, kids might suggest taking the person out to eat or to a movie. Have kids report back to the whole group what they brainstormed.

Group Shoulder Rub—To illustrate the nurturing effects of touch, have students stand in a circle and turn to the left. Have kids each massage the shoulders of the person in front of them. Then have kids turn to the right and repeat the procedure. Ask for reactions to the experience of touching and being touched. Ask how the experience might be different in a situation of helping a friend through grief.

FROM MOURNING

Below are the four "tasks" a grieving person must accomplish to grieve in a healthy way. Under each task, write practical things you could do to help a grieving friend accomplish the task. One or two ideas are listed for each task. With these ideas, you can help your friend move "from mourning to dancing."

1. The mourning person must accept the reality of the loss. People often would rather believe it didn't happen. To help, I could:

- Encourage my friend to talk about the facts of the loss (such as what, how, and when it happened).

- Encourage my friend to talk about the person who died.

-

-

2. The mourning person must experience the pain of grief. To help, I could:

- Allow my friend to show feelings of sadness, hurt or anger—even if those feelings don't seem appropriate to me.

-

-

3. The mourning person must learn to adjust to the new situation, without the person who died. To help, I could:

- Help my friend learn to do things that were usually done by the person who died.

-

-

4. The mourning person must put emotional energy into other relationships. To help, I could:

- Encourage my friend to participate with other friends in doing fun activities.

- Tell my friend about people available to offer love and support.

-

-

You can also bring a sense of hope to your friend. Read Revelation 21:1-4. Think of one way you can tell your friend about the message of this passage and write it below:

TO DANCING

LESSON 4

TO LIVE OR DIE

Few people deny the value of modern medicine. But medical science's improved techniques and technology have also created new debates. The biggest of these is the euthanasia debate.

Junior highers may be touched by the "right to die" controversy through stories in the news, discussions at school or knowing someone on life-support systems. With good biblical advice, kids can develop a balanced perspective on the issue.

LESSON AIM

To help junior highers explore the issue of euthanasia.

OBJECTIVES

Students will:
● identify the pros and cons of mercy killing;
● brainstorm ways to care for terminally ill people;
● explore what the Bible says about caring for others; and
● pledge to work at reaching out to people in need.

BIBLE BASIS

EXODUS 20:13
JOB 6:1-11

Look up the following scriptures. Then read the background paragraphs to see how the passages relate to your junior highers and middle schoolers.

Exodus 20:13 is a commandment not to kill.

God gave the Ten Commandments to the Israelites to show them the depth of his holiness. But the commandments were also practical rules for guiding the people who followed God.

Young teenagers may question whether there are moral absolutes in the world. Yet few would argue that murder is okay. In the right-to-die controversy, the question kids must answer is, "Is mercy killing murder?"

In **Job 6:1-11**, Job laments his painful suffering and wishes God would let him die.

In the midst of extreme pain, both emotional and physical, Job comes to where he only has one desire—to die. Job asks his friends why he should go on living.

What can we do when someone really wants to die? Job's experience could become a compelling argument for—or against—euthanasia. While it may seem that Job was asking his friends to help (or let) him die, he was actually asking God. Kids will need to explore this passage closely to come to their own understanding of who should be in control of someone's life.

THIS LESSON AT A GLANCE

Section	Minutes	What Students Will Do	Supplies
Opener (Option 1)	5 to 10	**Needle-Less Suffering**—Play a game to introduce the euthanasia issue.	Needles, thread
(Option 2)		**Hurtful or Helpful?**—Determine how they feel about euthanasia.	
Action and Reflection	10 to 15	**Slow Burn**—Experience a quick life-or-death situation and discuss the right to die.	Newsprint, tape, marker
Bible Application	10 to 15	**Contrasting Images**—Examine both sides of the euthanasia debate, using Bible passages to spark discussion.	Bibles, "Pros" and "Cons" boxes (p. 43)
Commitment	10 to 15	**What Does It Mean to Me?**—Complete a handout and discuss how they can respond to people who want to die.	"What Can I Do?" handouts (p. 45), pencils
Closing (Option 1)	up to 5	**Who Cares?**—Creatively show compassion for each other.	Construction paper, markers
(Option 2)		**Thank You**—Tell ways they've helped each other through painful times.	

Note: This lesson deals with the controversial topic of euthanasia (mercy killing). Before diving into the lesson, ask your senior pastor to explain your denomination's views on the issue. You'll also have a time during the Bible Application activity to discuss your denomination's views.

The Lesson

☐ OPTION 1: NEEDLE-LESS SUFFERING

Form pairs. Give each pair two needles and a strand of thread, at least 1 foot long. Say: **You'll each have a few opportunities to try to do something difficult that may cause pain or misery. Place your needles on the floor.**

OPENER
(5 to 10 minutes)

When I say "go," pick up the needles with one hand and put the thread through the eyes of both needles with your other hand. You must hold both needles between the finger and thumb of one hand. If you drop a needle, or if one hand touches the other, you'll be disqualified.

You'll have one minute to attempt this task. During that time, your partner must decide whether to let you continue trying to complete the task or to "put you out of your misery" by calling it quits. Your partner may not help you thread the needles. If you're "put out of your misery" before the time is up, you receive 3 points. If you fail to complete the task within the time limit, you won't get any points. If you successfully complete the task, you get 50 points.

Give partners each two attempts at the task. Then total the points for each pair and determine the winners. Don't forget to collect the needles.

Ask:

● **Was it easy to wait and not put your partner out of his or her misery during this game? Why or why not?** (Yes, I was hopeful my partner could thread the needles; no, I didn't think my partner could thread the needles.)

Say: **Watching someone struggle with a seemingly impossible task usually brings out feelings of pity and compassion in us. But is it more compassionate to allow them to keep trying? to help them? or to mercifully stop their suffering?**

This lesson deals with a tough issue: mercy killing, also referred to as euthanasia. Today we'll struggle with the issue of whether killing someone can ever be considered kinder than helping that person continue to live a painful life.

☐ OPTION 2: HURTFUL OR HELPFUL?

Form a circle. Have a volunteer step into the center of the circle, close both eyes, and fold his or her arms. Say: **Imagine that our volunteer is a pinball, and you're bumpers in a pinball machine.**

Have the volunteer wander blindly around the circle for a minute or so, bouncing off kids' outstretched arms. Remind kids to be gentle as they push the volunteer around the circle.

Afterward, ask the volunteer:

● **How did you feel as you were bounced around the circle?** (Uncomfortable; sore; confused.)

Say: **Today we're going to talk about an issue that's as difficult to handle as a pinball in a pinball machine. And, just as we bounced our pinball around the circle, we'll bounce this issue around until we better understand it. The issue is mercy killing, also known as euthanasia.**

Say: **I'll read aloud three statements. After each statement, you must respond with an action that identifies** how you feel about that statement. If you totally agree, stand up. If you're not sure how you feel, sit in a chair. If you totally disagree, sit on the floor.

First, let me set up a scene for you. Imagine the case of a 98-year-old woman who's in the hospital, dying of painful cancer. The woman has been given about a week to live. She has no relatives. A doctor offers her a glass of water, but the woman refuses to drink, saying: "It's time for me to die. I'm not going to eat or drink anymore. Please let me die."

Now respond to each of the following statements:

● Not to feed the woman would be murder, since it would kill her. The doctor should hook up intravenous feeding tubes.

● It would be kindest to go along with the woman's wishes, while making her as comfortable as possible.

● The doctor should assist the woman in a quick, painless death by immediately giving her a lethal dose of morphine.

After kids have responded, ask:

● **What did you notice about the way people responded to each statement?** (We all had the same responses; we didn't all agree.)

● **Is this an easy situation to deal with? Why or why not?** (Yes, the woman should be allowed to do what she wants; no, it's tough to know what's right.)

Say: **It's tough to know what's best to do for a person who seems to be in a hopeless situation. What's our duty as Christians in such situations? This lesson will focus on whether suffering should ever be considered more of an evil than dying.**

SLOW BURN

Ask a volunteer to be a character in a brief drama. Have the person sit in a chair at the front of the room. Lean another chair against the volunteer to simulate a smashed-in car door. Tell the group to pretend the volunteer has just been in a terrible car accident. The person is trapped in a car, and the car has just burst into flames. The volunteer can't get out, so he or she is being burned by the flames.

To the group, say: **As you drive to a friend's house, you come upon this scene. No one else is around. You can hear the person in the car screaming at you. The person begging you to shoot (him or her), because the pain is so great.** (Have the volunteer cry out for help and beg to be killed.)

You have a rifle in the trunk because you're going on a hunting trip. You have three options: (1) Do nothing and let the person die in the fire; (2) Try to help and risk your own life; or (3) Shoot.

Tell kids they have one minute to decide what they'll do,

ACTION AND REFLECTION
(10 to 15 minutes)

but they must unanimously agree, because as a group they represent one person. Say "go," then begin timing the kids. After 50 seconds, count aloud down to zero. Then have kids act out their decision.

After the decision is made, form a circle with the whole group and ask:

● **How did you feel about making this quick decision?** (I was anxious; I felt confused; I was unsure; I didn't like it.)

● **How is this situation like real life?** (It's tough to know what to do when someone's suffering; people don't agree on how to respond to tough issues like this.)

● **Which response to this situation would've been the most kind? Explain.** (Shooting the volunteer, because he or she wouldn't have to suffer; trying to help, because we might've been able to save the person.)

Ask kids to define "compassion." Write their ideas on a sheet of newsprint taped to the wall. Then have kids brainstorm "acts of compassion," such as caring for someone who's sick, feeding hungry animals, or helping a friend overcome grief. List these items on the newsprint.

Then say: **The euthanasia debate hinges on the question of what's both legal and compassionate. When someone who's terminally ill requests to be taken off life-support systems because of great pain, is it more compassionate to help the person die? or to hope for and attempt to provide for recovery?**

Ask:

● **Could killing ever be considered a form of kindness? Why or why not?** (Yes, if the suffering was too great; no, killing is always wrong.)

Say: **As Christians, we're called upon to be compassionate toward others. But what happens when our compassion conflicts with God's commandment not to kill? Let's take a look at what we can learn from the Bible to help us deal with this difficult situation.**

BIBLE APPLICATION
(10 to 15 minutes)

CONTRASTING IMAGES

Have a volunteer read aloud Exodus 20:13 and Job 6:1-11. Say: **Euthanasia is the act of causing death painlessly to end suffering. Some people support euthanasia as a way to help people dying of incurable, painful diseases. Others say it's murder.**

The two scriptures we just read present both sides of the debate. Job wants to die, but the Ten Commandments prohibit killing.

Ask:

● **How do these verses help us know how to respond to the issue of mercy killing?** (They don't; they only give us part of the big picture.)

Have someone read aloud Luke 10:36-37.

Ask:

● **What do these verses seem to suggest about mercy killing?** (Do what's merciful; take care of terminally ill people.)

Form two groups. Give a copy of the "Pros" list in the margin to one group and the "Cons" list to the other. Have groups stand opposite of each other, about 10 feet apart. Say: **When I say "go," groups will take turns reading aloud items from their lists. As you listen to each statement, think about whether you agree or disagree with it. If you agree with the other team's statement, take one large step toward the other group. If you disagree, stay where you are. You don't need to follow the other group members' actions. Think about how *you* feel and make *your own* decisions.**

Have groups alternate reading aloud one of their statements.

After the last statement is read, ask kids to look around at where everyone is standing.

Ask:

● **What surprised you most about the way people responded to these statements?** (We didn't all agree; we had similar responses.)

Say: **In this activity, we discovered the arguments for and against euthanasia. Both sides use scripture to support their arguments.**

At this time, present your denomination's views on euthanasia. Help kids understand why your church supports its specific beliefs. Then continue with the lesson.

Say: **One thing the Bible is clear on is how we can reach out to people who are terminally ill.**

WHAT DOES IT MEAN TO ME?

Say: **We may never be in a situation where we'll be asked to make a decision about euthanasia. But we'll probably have opportunities to respond to people suffering from terminal illnesses. How will we help?**

Give kids each a "What Can I Do?" handout (p. 45) and a pencil. Have kids each read and complete their handout. Then form groups of no more than four. Have kids each share their brainstormed ideas in their groups. Then have groups each choose the three best ideas to tell the class.

Have representatives from each group tell the class their ideas. Have kids vote on one or more ideas to put into action during the coming weeks. Help coordinate the ideas as necessary and be sure to follow up on kids' actions.

Pros

1. Death would be an act of kindness for people who have incurable diseases and are in great pain.

2. Some people prefer death to a life of pain or unconsciousness.

3. Minimizing suffering is always a kind thing to do.

4. Euthanasia helps people keep their dignity; keeping them alive might make them burdens on society.

5. Euthanasia lives up to the good Samaritan ideal because it helps people in need.

- -

Cons

1. God's commandment says killing is always wrong.

2. Euthanasia removes the possibility of a miraculous recovery.

3. Prolonging life is always a kind thing to do.

4. Maintaining human dignity is never more important than maintaining human life.

5. The good Samaritan ideal means doing all possible to maintain life while alleviating suffering.

COMMITMENT
(10 to 15 minutes)

Form a circle. Have volunteers read aloud their letters. Don't force kids to read them aloud, but encourage them each to read at least a portion of their letter.

Encourage kids to each send their letter to someone who has a terminal illness.

CLOSING
(up to 5 minutes)

☐ OPTION 1: WHO CARES?

Form a circle. Give kids each a sheet of construction paper and a marker. Say: **We can practice showing compassion to suffering people by showing love to each other. Think of something you appreciate about the person on your left. Write that on your construction paper. Then think of something you can do to show that person your compassion. For example, you might consider giving that person a hug, helping that person with schoolwork or taking that person out for ice cream. On your paper, write what you'll do for that person to show compassion during the coming week. Then present your paper to the person.**

Have kids each silently read the paper they're given. Then close in prayer, thanking God for giving us compassionate hearts, and seeking his guidance on the issue of euthanasia.

☐ OPTION 2: THANK YOU

Ask kids to think of ways they've helped each other through difficult or painful times. Have kids go around and thank each other for their specific efforts. Express your own thanks to each student for his or her willingness to be involved in this difficult course.

Form a circle and have volunteers describe times others have shown them compassion. Then close in prayer, asking God for wisdom about the euthanasia issue and giving thanks for his compassion.

If You Still Have Time . . .

Last Request—Ask kids to imagine they're suffering from a terminal illness and are in great pain.

Ask:

● **Would you choose to be given a lethal injection rather than suffer the pain? Why or why not?**

Ask kids to imagine they're unconscious and being kept alive only by artificial means.

Ask:

● **Would you want someone to "pull the plug" rather than hope for your slim chance of recovery? Why or why not?**

Have kids discuss the differences in these two scenarios.

Course Reflection—Form a circle. Ask students to reflect on the past four lessons. Have them take turns completing the following sentences:

● Something I learned in this course was . . .

● If I could tell my friends about this course, I'd say . . .

● Something I'll do differently because of this course is . . .

What Can I Do?

Much of the suffering of dying people comes from loneliness and lack of companionship. In the space to the right, list ways you could help someone who's suffering from loneliness due to illness.

Then, in the letter space, write to someone who's dying from cancer or another terminal illness. If you don't know of anyone who's terminally ill, write the letter to terminally ill people in general. Be sincere in what you say. Read Psalm 31:24 and John 5:24 for ideas on what you might say.

Ways I could help . . .

BONUS IDEAS

Unique Undertaking—Take your class on a field trip to a funeral home. Get parents' permission for kids to take the tour. Ask the funeral director to give a tour of the facility and explain what services are offered. Encourage kids to ask questions during the tour. After the tour, meet to discuss kids' feelings.

Graveside Gathering—Visit a cemetery with your kids. Give kids guidance about proper cemetery etiquette, such as no running, shouting, or walking over graves. Have kids read the tombstones and try to find the oldest person who died; the youngest person who died; the earliest date of death; and the latest date of death. If the cemetery allows, have kids do tombstone rubbings by placing large sheets of newsprint over the epitaphs and rubbing charcoal or crayons lightly over them. This way, your group will have written records of their findings.

While in the cemetery, have a brief prayer time, asking God to give the kids long, fruitful lives and confidence to face death with the hope of resurrection. Afterward, meet to discuss how kids felt in the cemetery.

Hospice Helper—Invite a volunteer hospice worker to give a short presentation to your group. Ask the volunteer to tell about experiences of helping the terminally ill and their families. Allow time for kids to ask questions about the grief process.

Suicide Isn't a Solution—Invite a pastor or counselor to talk with the group about the warning signs of people who are considering suicide and how to help them. Use the following checklist to begin discussion about suicide:

Suicide Warning Signs:

- Depression
- Aggression
- Excessive fantasizing
- Recent experience of loss
- Loss of pleasure
- Guilt
- Giving away possessions
- Comments about suicide (direct or indirect)
- Excessive risk-taking
- Failing grades

Encourage kids to watch for friends who may have some of these signs. Have the counselor or pastor suggest ways to help suicidal kids regain their desire to live.

Lethal Lyrics—Ask kids to bring cassettes or CDs that include songs about death. Listen to a few of the songs and have kids evaluate the lyrics in light of Christian beliefs.

Table Talk—Use the "Table Talk" handout (p. 20) as the basis for a meeting with parents and kids. Open the meeting with fun crowdbreakers to relax kids and parents before diving into this serious topic together. Check out *Quick Crowdbreakers and Games for Youth Groups* (Group Books) for fun ideas. Have parents and kids complete the handout together and then meet as one group to discuss what they discovered. Invite a pastor to attend and give his or her perspective about grieving, euthanasia and what happens after people die.

At the Funeral—Give kids each an "At the Funeral" handout (p. 48) and a pencil. Have kids complete the handout and discuss it. The statements lend themselves to role-plays, so if time permits, have kids act out scenes using helpful and not-so-helpful statements and actions. Encourage kids who've attended funerals to tell about their experiences.

Life-After-Death Party—Help kids plan a party to celebrate God's gift of eternal life. Decorate the room with colorful streamers and balloons to emphasize the joy of resurrection. When kids arrive, have the lights off in the room. Introduce the party by saying: **Eventually we'll all die. But when we become Christians, we're given a fantastic gift—life after death!** Turn on the lights and let the party begin.

Include a time of lively singing and game-playing. During the party, have kids each say one reason they're glad they're alive, and the first thing they'd like to ask God when they meet him face to face.

PARTY PLEASER

Compassion Retreat—Have a retreat where kids can learn to be compassionate toward each other and toward people who are suffering or grieving. Invite a professional counselor or a pastor to lead sessions on helping friends overcome the loss of a loved one. Include activities where kids can experience loss and talk about their feelings. Have kids describe how a loss experience can help them know how to reach out to others. Be sure to have fun times for games and singing too. Focus on the joy kids can bring to each other by showing their love and compassion.

RETREAT IDEA

AT THE FUNERAL

Checkmark the actions or words that seem unhelpful or inappropriate at a funeral. Put a star by actions or words that seem helpful.

_____ Say "But you still have your other (son, daughter, parent, grandparent, friends)."

_____ Talk about something other than the death; be as cheerful as possible.

_____ Invite the grieving person to tell how he or she feels.

_____ Tell all about the last funeral you attended.

_____ Stand silently beside a grieving friend, perhaps with a hand on his or her shoulder.

_____ Say "Please don't cry; you're going to make me cry."

_____ Complain about how the funeral director failed to provide adequate service.

_____ Say "At least (he or she) didn't suffer, right?"

_____ Offer a tissue to someone who's crying.

_____ Ask "How much did the insurance pay?"

_____ Let yourself feel the sadness of the occasion.

_____ Offer to pray with someone.

_____ Offer to provide child care while people visit with the family of the person who died.